a pocke
RHYME
Imagination for a new generation

2006 Poetry Competition for 7-11 year-olds

YoungWriters

Co Derry, Down & Fermanagh
Edited by Michelle Afford

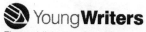 Young**Writers**

First published in Great Britain in 2007 by:
Young Writers
Remus House
Coltsfoot Drive
Peterborough
PE2 9JX
Telephone: 01733 890066
Website: www.youngwriters.co.uk

SB ISBN 1 84602 753 5

Foreword

Young Writers was established in 1991 and has been passionately devoted to the promotion of reading and writing in children and young adults ever since. The quest continues today. Young Writers remains as committed to the nurturing of poetic and literary talent as ever.

This year's Young Writers competition has proven as vibrant and dynamic as ever and we are delighted to present a showcase of the best poetry from across the UK and in some cases overseas. Each poem has been selected from a wealth of *A Pocketful Of Rhyme* entries before ultimately being published in this, our fourteenth primary school poetry series.

Once again, we have been supremely impressed by the overall quality of the entries we have received. The imagination, energy and creativity which has gone into each young writer's entry made choosing the poems a challenging and often difficult but ultimately hugely rewarding task - the general high standard of the work submitted ensured this opportunity to bring their poetry to a larger appreciative audience.

We sincerely hope you are pleased with this final collection and that you will enjoy *A Pocketful Of Rhyme Co Derry, Down & Fermanagh* for many years to come.

Contents

Carryduff Primary School, Belfast

Christopher Lamont (9)   1
Aaron Waddell (8)   2
Jonathan Brown (8)   3
Lewis Bell (8)   4
Alice Simpson (9)   5
Hannah McIlwrath (8)   6
Chloe Stranaghan (9)   7
Lucy Taylor (8)   8
Olivia Casement (8)   9
Erin Moorcroft (8)   10
Laura Finn (9)   11
Ellen Martin (9)   12
David Campbell (9)   13

Downpatrick Primary School, Downpatrick

Richard Hamilton (10)   14
Ryan Swail (10)   15
Adam Lynn (9)   16
Brittany Mills   17
Anna Kahla (9)   18
Christina Rea (9)   19
Georgia Fermor (9)   20
Matthew James Lennon (10)   21
Katy Clements (9)   22
Jenny King (9)   23
James Ferguson (10)   24
Maeve Anderson (10)   25

Gortnaghey Primary School, Dungiven

Jemma McElhinney (8)   26
Saoirise McElhinney (8)   27
Jonathan Moore (9)   28
Gabriel Farren (10)   29
Christopher McLaughlin (10)   30
Danny Mulhern (11)   31
Corey O'Reilly (9)   32

Newbuildings Primary School, Londonderry

Zahra Stewart (8)	33
Jodie McGregor (9)	34
Jamie Faulkner (9)	35
Sarah Davis (9)	36
Mason Pyper (8)	37
Dylan Hughes (8)	38
Ascott Long (9)	39
Abbie Colhoun (8)	40
Courtney Hughes (8)	41
Chelsea Black (9)	42
Ross Killen (8)	43
Lucy Olphert (8)	44
Luke Smyth (8)	45
Melissa Hamilton (9)	46
Rebecca Taylor (9)	47
Natalie Hunter (8)	48
Kristen Glenn (8)	49
Jessica McVeigh (8)	50

St Colman's Abbey Primary School, Newry

Eoghan Campbell (9)	51
Aaron Byrne (9)	52
Keith Kelly (10)	53
Daryl Bogues (9)	54
Ruairi Gorman (9)	55
David McKevitt (10)	56
Ross Haughey (9)	57
Paul Curran (9)	58
Joshua O'Brien (9)	59
Conall Keenan Reilly (9)	60
Niall Grant (9)	61
Garrett Campbell (10)	62
Anthony McKeown (10)	63
Jonathan McEvoy (9)	64
Gary McAleavey (9)	65
Daniel McNulty (10)	66

St Davog's Primary School, Belleek

Rachel O'Shea (9)	67
Nessa Rooney (8)	68

Kelly Louise Ferguson (8)	69
Michael Óg McGarrigle (7)	70
Lauren Doogan (7)	71
Caoimhe Rooney (8)	72
Joanne Murphy (8)	73
Eve Rochfort (9)	74
Arlene Cassidy (10)	75
Aidan Murphy (10)	76
Conor Murphy (10)	77
Shane Edward Mimna (10)	78
Maeve Lunny (11)	79
Ethan McGrath (9)	80
Nathan Hanley (9)	81
Shane Rooney (9)	82
Caoimhe McGarrigle (10)	83
Peter Gilfedder (10)	84
Saoirse O'Loughlin (10)	85

St Martin's Primary School, Garrison

JJ O'Brien (10)	86
Fearghal Kelly (10)	87
John Burns (9)	88
Aisling McGurl (8)	89
Michelle Keegan-Rattcliff (9)	90
Laura Keegan-Rattcliff (9)	91
Ciara McGrath (8)	92
Connor Chappell (7)	93
Oisin O'Brien (6)	94
Katie Stewart (7)	95
Catie Wadsworth (7)	96
Chloe McGrath (6)	97
Jonah Carty (7)	98
Sinead McGurl (7)	99
Cianna Treacy (7)	100
Lauren Timoney (6)	101
Tony Devine (7)	102
Tristan Otto (7)	103
Lorena McIntyre (8)	104
Jarlath O'Brien (8)	105
Meghan McTernan (8)	106
Mairéad Maguire (8)	107

James Keown (8)   108
Darren Carson (8)   109
Fiona Keegan (8)   110
Darragh Treacy (8)   111
Darragh Ferguson (8)   112

St Mary's Primary School Dechomet, Castlewellan

Ciaran McElroy (6)   113
Cahal Owens (6)   114
Katie Doyle (6)   115
Mollie Cunningham (6)   116
Caoimhe Leneghan (6)   117
Matthew Leneghan (6)   118
Tiarnan McEvoy (7)   119
Ciaran McElroy (7)   120
Carlin Mooney (7)   121
Kathryn Kelly (10)   122
Claire Cunningham (7)   123
Paul Savage (7)   124
Shaneen Owens (7)   125
Tiernan O'Rourke (7)   126
Pearse Davidson (7)   127
Shea O'Boyle (8)   128
Peirce Laverty (8)   129
Conor McQuillan (8)   130
Caitlin Owens (8)   131
Eve Cunningham (8)   132
Claire Greeran (8)   133
Jane Doyle (8)   134
Katie Rose Thornton (9)   135
James Savage (9)   136
Ryan Cunningham (9)   137
PJ Davidson (9)   138
Paddy McEvoy (10)   139
Aiden O'Hare (10)   140
Sean Óg O'Rourke (10)   141
Aaron Owens (10)   142
Peter McEvoy (10)   143
Shana O'Boyle (10)   144
Claren Owens (10)   145
Megan Owens (10)   146

Natasha McQuillan (10)   147
Erin Leneghan (11)   148
Michael O'Rourke (11)   149

The Irish Society's Primary School, Coleraine

Sarah Sim (10)   150
Rebecca Sim (10)   151
Charlotte Warke (10)   152
Hayley Gibson (10)   153
Shareffa Walker (10)   154
Sarah Young (10)   155
Adam Gellatly (11)   156
Jordan Moore (11)   157
Demi Quinn (10)   158
Abigail Sharp (10)   159
Jack Friel (10)   160
Danni Millar (11)   161
Olivia Clarke (10)   162
Bradley Dempster (10)   163
Aaruj Akbar (11)   164
Rachael Thompson (11)   165
Mahnoor Tughral (11)   166
Jade McMaster (10)   167
John Gordon (11)   168
Tori Cameron (11)   169
Duncan Chapman (10)   170
Jonathan Kennedy (10)   171
Faine Eustace (11)   172
Cara Ferguson (11)   173
Hannah Gibson (10)   174
Sarah Boyles (10)   175
Reuben Simpson (10)   176
Jamie Rosborough (10)   177
Megan Downs (10)   178
Naomi Hazel Wray (10)   179
Clarice Friel (10)   180
Yasmin Macauley (11)   181
Emma Clarke (10)   182
Amy Taylor (10)   183
Victoria Irwin (11)   184
Alex Skuce (10)   185

Stephen Coulter (11)   186
Andrew William Coulter (11)   187
Jakob Henry Gault Allen (10)   188
Kurtis Thompson (10)   189
Peter Culkin (10)   190
Matthew Thomas Wisener (10)   191
Joel Stanbridge (11)   192
Kate Hewitt (10)   193
Sarah Henning (11)   194
Jenny Clarke (10)   195
James Hemphill (10)   196
Shane McMullan (11)   197
Hayley McMullan (10)   198
Claire Cooper (11)   199

The Poems

Coke

Coke is made from sugary sweetness.
I found it in the freezer,
But my dog had been there first.

My dog is drinking my Coke,
I didn't know my dog liked Coke,
I thought it was amazing!

I could not believe it,
So I had to clean it up,
I had to buy a new box of Coke.

So I got a bottle instead of a tin,
Because my dog can't open
The lid with his paws.

Christopher Lamont (9)
Carryduff Primary School, Belfast

There Was A Boy With Very Long Hair

There was a boy with very long hair,
It would never stop growing,
When he was cutting his hair,
The scissors would not cut through,
The hair just grew thicker,
The scissors would break,
One day it grew and grew and grew,
Then it poured with rain,
Everyone looked at the boy,
His hair had grown up into the clouds.

Aaron Waddell (8)
Carryduff Primary School, Belfast

Seasons

I like trees because they sway in the breeze
I like leaves because they crackle on the ground
I think the sun is as bright as a light
I think the snow is as cold as ice
I think clouds look like cotton wool
To get rid of rain, let it pour down your drain
I like puddles because you can splash in them
I like all seasons because they're all fun.

Jonathan Brown (8)
Carryduff Primary School, Belfast

The Weather

When the weather is sunny - it feels nice and warm
When the weather is rainy - it feels all soggy and damp
When the weather is sunny and rainy - there may be a rainbow
When the weather is snowy - it is lots of fun
When the weather is foggy - it is hard to see
When the weather is stormy - it is hard to hear people
When the weather is windy - it is usually cold
When the weather is hot - it is roasting
When the weather is freezing - you should stay indoors
When there is a slight breeze - it is breezy
When there is some thunder - it is thundery
When I am asleep there are sometimes showers.

Lewis Bell (8)
Carryduff Primary School, Belfast

Snow

Snow is white -
It is very soft.
I like it best -
If snow is cold.

Snow appears in winter,
I can have snowball fights.
Snow is fun,
I can make a snowman.

Sometimes I see snowflakes,
I can lie in the snow -
Make snow angels with me?

Alice Simpson (9)
Carryduff Primary School, Belfast

Colours

Colours are red, blue, black
Colours are beautiful and so are you
Colours can make you go to sleep
Some of the colours are like the sky
Colours floating in the air
Colours are as beautiful as flowers
Colours are all around you
Colours are on the animals.

Hannah McIlwrath (8)
Carryduff Primary School, Belfast

Flowers, Flowers

Flowers - I like them a lot,
Flowers - put them in a pot,
Flowers - they smell nice,
Flowers - beyond price.

Roses are my favourite flowers,
Flowers make me smile a lot,
Flowers - make me gleam,
Flowers - make me sing,
I love gardens full of flowers.

Chloe Stranaghan (9)
Carryduff Primary School, Belfast

Flowers, Flowers

Flowers, flowers - I like the lot
Flowers, flowers - put them in a pot
Flowers, flowers - they smell nice
Flowers, flowers - beyond price.
Roses are my favourite flowers.
Flowers make me smile a lot
Flowers, flowers - make me gleam
Flowers, flowers - make me sing
I love gardens full of flowers, flowers.

Lucy Taylor (8)
Carryduff Primary School, Belfast

Colours

Colours are more than red and blue
Colours are all around you.
Colours are in the sky
Colours are on your houses.
Colours are on your shoes
Roses are red and so is your face.
Colours are on your pets
And colours are all over you.

Olivia Casement (8)
Carryduff Primary School, Belfast

Colours

Some colours are red, black and blue,
Colours are pretty and so are you.

Colours can make you go to sleep,
Colours are like the sky floating in the air.

Colours are such beautiful things,
Colours are even in your dreams.

There are colours in the air,
Colours like grey and black are very dull.

Erin Moorcroft (8)
Carryduff Primary School, Belfast

Homework

All the children in my class
Don't like homework.
I also agree
No matter what it is
They have to do it.
A world with no homework . . .
I think of in my dreams.
But the worst thing is
When I wake up
It's just a dream.
Then I nearly burst into tears
There's still homework left in the world.

Laura Finn (9)
Carryduff Primary School, Belfast

The Alphabet To M

A is for apples that fall from trees
B is for bees that make us honey
C is for candy that is so sweet
D is for bright yellow daffodils
E is for explosions that are very loud
F is for fire, keeps me warm on cold winter nights
G is for tall giraffes that are yellow with brown spots
H is for happiness that flows around the world
I is for illness that spreads throughout the universe
J is for jumpers that keep you warm and cosy
K is for kangaroos that keep their joeys in their pouches
L is for love that can last forever if you treasure it
M is for mothers that will love you forever.

Ellen Martin (9)
Carryduff Primary School, Belfast

The Sea Monster

There was a monster from the sea.
Here's what we had for our tea.
I ate chips and he ate ships,
I ate bread and he ate a seal's head.
But Monster was lonely.
He had no friends,
He was born in the River Thames.

David Campbell (9)
Carryduff Primary School, Belfast

Harvest

H is for hunger spread around the world
A is for apples that grow on the trees
R is for ripe fruits
V is for vegetables that keep you healthy
E is for the ears of corn harvested by the farmers
S is for scattered seeds
T is for tractors ploughing the ground.

Richard Hamilton (10)
Downpatrick Primary School, Downpatrick

Harvest

Harvest is traditional and happens every year
Wintertime is drawing near
The gentle swaying of the wheat
That makes the bread that we eat
Families prepare the harvest meal
The golden crops farmers must conceal
Before the rain the fields are still
Around the tables children eat their fill
Families sing and pray with cheer
When harvest comes around each year.

Ryan Swail (10)
Downpatrick Primary School, Downpatrick

The Harvest Of God

Golden wheat swaying
Like the sunlight on the waves
The reaper comes and slices it
Like a knife through butter

Green apple grain is packed away
In store and stall
Flaming furnaces roar
Ready for baking bread

God watches through the clouds
Pleased with the harvest.

Adam Lynn (9)
Downpatrick Primary School, Downpatrick

Harvest

Harvest is the best
Harvest is cool
Harvest is the one
Harvest is the best one in the world
I like harvest now it is here today
I am happy now
Harvest is here.

Brittany Mills
Downpatrick Primary School, Downpatrick

Harvest Time

As the farmer ploughs his fields
His wife gathers an abundance of yellow grain
Vroom goes the tractor as it drives past the windmills
Bumping over the hills
The flowers sway then are picked and bunched to sell
Lots of different fruits are being boxed and sold
As it's getting dark, now the diesel in the tractor starts to run out
The sun is going down
Now they settle down to a table of fruit and vegetables for tea
As they enjoy they give a toast of thanks
For the beautiful crop they have received
Sky turns black, harvest ends happily!

Anna Kahla (9)
Downpatrick Primary School, Downpatrick

Harvest

The wheat sways in the wind, ready to be gathered,
The golden ears ever so bright.
The tractor comes rumbling with a plough on the back
And plucks every one of them out.
The fruits, round and juicy, are found high on a bush,
They glisten in our fruit bowls and taste of delight.
Thank you, Lord, for all our gifts on this Harvest Day,
Teach us to appreciate all You send our way.

Christina Rea (9)
Downpatrick Primary School, Downpatrick

Harvest Poem

H arvest, a beautiful time of year
A nd every fruit is ripe and juicy
R eady golden corn sways in the wind
V illages with views of wheat fields
E veryone smiling when the job is done
S unsets shine on scurrying squirrels
T ime for tired farmers to take a rest.

Georgia Fermor (9)
Downpatrick Primary School, Downpatrick

Is This What Harvest Is About?

The sweet taste of blackberries,
The heads of golden corn,
The rosy red apples,
The wind in my hair,
Is this what harvest's about?

Up come the poppies,
Down go the leaves,
As the squirrel buries his nuts,
Is this what harvest's about?

As the combine harvester slows
And the tractor rides back to the yard,
With the wheat stacked high,
Is this what harvest's about?

All of these things are harvest,
But the thing that you must understand,
Is that harvest's a time of thanksgiving,
Thanksgiving, for you and me.

Matthew James Lennon (10)
Downpatrick Primary School, Downpatrick

Harvest

H appily gathering in the crops
A bundant is the fruit
R ipening on the trees
V ery laden with flavour
E veryone is happy and caring
S owing the new seeds
T his is all thanks to the Lord.

Katy Clements (9)
Downpatrick Primary School, Downpatrick

The Harvest

It's harvest time again,
The heavy combine reaps,
It cuts down the corn before the rain,
Nowhere left for the mice to sleep.

It's harvest time again,
Branches heavy with abundant fruits,
Rosy apples, juicy pears, we will gain,
Run and get your boots.

It's harvest time again,
No slashing scythes, no creaking carts,
Tractors have ploughed and reaped the bigger plains,
Summer has ended, autumn starts.

Jenny King (9)
Downpatrick Primary School, Downpatrick

Harvest Poem

Harvest is fun, exciting and hard work
We wouldn't have a lot to eat, if the farmers weren't here
They grow corn, wheat, vegetables and fruit
Harvest time is when we celebrate what the farmers have grown
We can get fruit, flowers or vegetables to give to other people
We thank the Lord that He created farmers
The farmers collect the grain to make flour for our bread
The farmer grows fruit and veg for us to eat.

James Ferguson (10)
Downpatrick Primary School, Downpatrick

Harvest

H elping poor people is really easy
A t harvest we help others by giving gifts
R aising money is where we come in to help
V isiting people who you are helping
E nergy is put into it
S tarving people will get a better life
T o make them have a better life.

Maeve Anderson (10)
Downpatrick Primary School, Downpatrick

Feeling Peckish

My cat is very, very greedy
One day, she will turn into a horse
Though she will not be very speedy
She is very, very fat
She likes to play with her mat.

Jemma McElhinney (8)
Gortnaghey Primary School, Dungiven

School

I like school
It's so cool
At break time I run
And do cool stuff.

I like to play with my friends
Until it all ends
At the swimming pool
It is also cool.

But I like art the best
I don't know about the rest
This is why I like school.

Saoirise McElhinney (8)
Gortnaghey Primary School, Dungiven

I Live In A House

I live in a house
One day I saw a mouse
And it had a long body
And a curly tail
And I watched it eat a snail.

I reached for the broom
And I swept it out of the room
I hope it doesn't come back
Too soon!

Jonathan Moore (9)
Gortnaghey Primary School, Dungiven

School

My school is cool
Because I go to the pool
At break time I have fun
Because I run
So don't be a fool
Go to school
Because we have a new teacher
Mrs Duffy is her name
And we have new P1s and this year
Is going to be a busy year.

Gabriel Farren (10)
Gortnaghey Primary School, Dungiven

Playing At School

My school is really very cool
Because I go to the swimming pool
At break time I play with my friends round the school
They are cool
I sometimes play football at school
My school is lovely and good
And I especially like the food
So go to school, don't be a fool.

Christopher McLaughlin (10)
Gortnaghey Primary School, Dungiven

My Pet Reno

My pet is a pup called Reno
He's small and sweet
With four tiny white feet
Everyone I meet
Thinks he's quiet neat.

I walk him each day
He's crazy
And he loves to play.

When I tuck him in at night
I know he will wake up
Cheery and bright.

Danny Mulhern (11)
Gortnaghey Primary School, Dungiven

The Windmills

The windmills on the mountain
Twenty-one there are and all,
Standing close together
Straight, white and tall

They wave to every person
Whether walking or in a car
'Cause you can see these windmills
From very near or very far
There's one special windmill
Which belongs to my friend, Niamh
It will turn forever
And her memory will never leave

They look down on Gortnaghey
And wave to us as we play
Saying, 'Behave and be good
And have a lovely day!'

Corey O'Reilly (9)
Gortnaghey Primary School, Dungiven

Anger

Anger is red like a fiery flame going up
It looks like the Big Bad Wolf
It tastes like wooch, booch, gooch goo,
It sounds like a roaring tiger
It reminds me of the big monster of the deep
It feels like wooch, sticky, runny goo
It makes me feel scared
It smells like runny, gooey, squishy poo.

Zahra Stewart (8)
Newbuildings Primary School, Londonderry

Anger

Anger smells like a flaming hot, ugly devil jumping out of my skin
It looks like a spiky, smoky fireball
It tastes like green, sludgy, moulded-up carrots from last week's dinner
It sounds like a terrifying, dirty, monstrous zombie calling from

                                                    the dead

It reminds me of a tall vampire covered in warts
Coming to suck my brains out of my head
It is red like blood running out of my veins.

Jodie McGregor (9)
Newbuildings Primary School, Londonderry

Hate

It sounds like screaming and scratching
Like a scorpion screeching
It looks like a muddy, messy mummy just raised from the dead
It feels like a slimy, mushy, crusty piece of slime
It smells like sheep dung and it's all mushy and gooey
It reminds me of a blood-sucking devil
Sucking blood out of my head and eating my eyeballs
It makes me feel like I'm on fire and being run over by a lorry
It sounds like your waxy, disgusting eardrums bursting
With the loud banging of a drum.

Jamie Faulkner (9)
Newbuildings Primary School, Londonderry

Loneliness

It is like your best friend is leaving you for an enemy
It makes me feel as if I am locked in a tower
And have been a prisoner for one hundred years
It tastes like someone daring you to eat salty, slushy, enormous poo
It looks like a cute, cuddly kitten
Getting run over by a large green tractor
It reminds you of someone telling you you're in pain
And attacking you
It smells like someone who hasn't taken a shower for a year
The colour of it is ruby-red, with a hint of black!

Sarah Davis (9)
Newbuildings Primary School, Londonderry

Anger

Anger is like blood pouring out of your heart
It sounds like a big-eared elephant roaring in my ear
Sometimes I feel like howling up to the moon
It tastes like Brussels sprouts that have been made for two weeks
It smells like Frankenstein, with rats and poison on the table
It reminds me of my great gran.

Mason Pyper (8)
Newbuildings Primary School, Londonderry

Anger

It puts me off when I'm doing my work, when I put up my hand
It tastes like someone stuffing hard wood into my mouth
It feels like squishy, slimy, slushy yellow goo
It sounds like the red, roaring Devil roaring in my ear
It looks like pumping rides coming towards me like a ghost spirit
It reminds me of the flaming, fiery sunshine in my eyes
It's dark, dark black with red and blue stripes
It makes me feel like I've been put in the kettle
For a cup of warm coffee.

Dylan Hughes (8)
Newbuildings Primary School, Londonderry

Anger

Anger is red like a big, blazing, hot fire
It sounds like steam firing out of my ears
It looks like my daddy after work
It feels like I have everything to do myself
It reminds me of my sister and her room
It tastes like my cousin on the toilet
It makes me feel like I have cats all around me.

Ascott Long (9)
Newbuildings Primary School, Londonderry

Hate

It feels like I am going to explode into little pieces
It smells like rotten onions
It reminds me of getting angry when my brother lied to me
It looks like a devil at Hallowe'en time
The colour is black like smoke
It makes me feel very angry
It tastes like burnt sausages
It sounds like the fire alarm bursting out its sound.

Abbie Colhoun (8)
Newbuildings Primary School, Londonderry

Love

Love is a lovely bright red with pink hearts
Love sounds like a little bird singing in my ear
Love reminds me of my baby sister
Love feels like a nice, fluffy pillow
Love looks like a big bubble of hearts
Love makes me feel like I am falling into a pool of love
Love smells like a sweet bunch of red roses
Love tastes like a lovely apple pie.

Courtney Hughes (8)
Newbuildings Primary School, Londonderry

Happiness

Happiness is the colour of blue and fills me with happiness
It tastes like a rainbow in my path and the sea in my body
It makes me feel like butterflies are in my tummy
It reminds me of the sunshine in the sky
It looks like butterflies in the sky
It makes me feel like the sun is beating down on me
It smells like rain beating down on me
It looks like birds flying away.

Chelsea Black (9)
Newbuildings Primary School, Londonderry

Love

It reminds me of the time I said I love school
It makes me feel like getting a kiss from my mummy
It sounds like a kiss from my mummy
It is the colour of my mummy's lips
It tastes like a lovely fried egg
It smells like a strawberry.

Ross Killen (8)
Newbuildings Primary School, Londonderry

Being Excluded

Being excluded is clear, like nobody can hear me or see me
Only myself, it's like I don't exist
It feels like everybody else is inside a beautiful, bright place
And I'm locked outside, alone in a horrible, pitch-dark
Terrible place with nothing in it
It smells like the horrible eggy, stinky smell when my mum
Opens the smelly dishwasher
It looks like a family has just pushed me out
And abandoned me, lonely and stranded
It sounds like arguing and fighting, deadly lions roaring terribly
It reminds me of the horrible, heartbreaking, family-splitting tsunami
It tastes like stuck-together, mouldy, out-of-date
Horrible chicken fried rice.

Lucy Olphert (8)
Newbuildings Primary School, Londonderry

Anger

Anger smells like disgusting things
Like out-of-date mild, mouldy cheese and slimy diarrhoea
It feels like a German has shot me in the head
It makes me feel as if I was eaten by a man-eating lizard
It sounds like a monstrous roar that goes on forever
It looks like a monster that won't leave me alone
It reminds me of a fire-breathing dragon
Anger could be any colour, like a multicoloured snake
It tastes like out-of-date cheese.

Luke Smyth (8)
Newbuildings Primary School, Londonderry

Sadness

Sadness makes me feel like nothing can change
It sounds like silence throughout the world
It is black like a deep, dark hole that never ends
It feels like you're falling down that deep, dark hole that never ends
It tastes like burnt gammon stuck in your mouth
It smells like a cake that has just exploded in the oven
It looks like a heart being ripped in two.

Melissa Hamilton (9)
Newbuildings Primary School, Londonderry

Love

Love is red like a heart
It sounds like your heart is beating
It feels like you're standing on top of the sun
It smells like fresh flowers from the field
It reminds me of my cousin, Sam, when he was born
It tastes like all my vegetables
It looks like my teacher when she comes into class
In her beautiful clothes.

Rebecca Taylor (9)
Newbuildings Primary School, Londonderry

Happiness

It feels like the world is full of happiness
It smells like the breeze and the fresh air
It tastes like lemon juice and it is nice and cool
It looks like the sun and the sea
It reminds me of a colourful rainbow
And wind blowing on me and it is beautiful
It makes me feel happy and proud
It sounds like people chatting happily with their friends
It is gorgeous bright pink with light blue.

Natalie Hunter (8)
Newbuildings Primary School, Londonderry

Loneliness

It makes me feel like nobody knows me
It sounds like a plane going very fast in the air
It smells like my cat's litter tray
It is a very light pink
It reminds me of when my fish called Goldy died
It looks like my kitten curled up
It tastes like brown sauce.

Kristen Glenn (8)
Newbuildings Primary School, Londonderry

Inside My Heart

It sounds like a monkey clawing in my hair
It reminds me of when my mum gave me a cookie
It feels like a slushy board
My heart is red like an apple-shaped as a heart
It makes me feel like I am loved forever
It looks like a nose, as sharp as a heart
It smells like a beautiful, buzzing butterfly
It tastes like a rotten boiled egg out of a microwave.

Jessica McVeigh (8)
Newbuildings Primary School, Londonderry

A Sunny Day

Oh, sun, sun, you are so hot,
Hotter than a boiling pot,
You're strong and bright,
You make the birds tweet
And make their singing, oh so sweet!

Oh, sun, sun, you make the grass grow,
You even help the rivers flow,
I like the way you make the animals speak,
You make frogs croak, bees hum,
Every day of the week.

Eoghan Campbell (9)
St Colman's Abbey Primary School, Newry

The Summer Sun

On this lovely summer's day,
We can't wait to go out and play,
In the beautiful clear blue sky,
The birds are skimming, oh so high!

Ice cream's the food you want to eat,
While relaxing on your colourful summer seat,
The barbecue is hot, the drinks are cool,
Kids are splashing in the paddling pool.

The sun is setting, the sky is red,
It's time for me to go to bed.

Aaron Byrne (9)
St Colman's Abbey Primary School, Newry

The Tree

Oh mighty tree,
You stand so tall,
With branches as your arms.

You have no legs
So you cannot move
When you hear the woodcutter's call
It's your time to fall.

Keith Kelly (10)
St Colman's Abbey Primary School, Newry

A Bright Summer Day

It was a bright summer's day
So I thought I would go away
I got up, got changed
Then got packed up for a day at the beach
When I got there
I could feel a warm breeze
I went looking for a place to fish
I caught some fish
Put them on the grill of the BBQ
Ate them and said
'I will come back next year.'

Daryl Bogues (9)
St Colman's Abbey Primary School, Newry

Rain In My Garden

I longed to go out to the garden
But it had rained for two weeks
Rain fell silently
I could hear birds tweet.

The rain did stop
But was still too wet to go out
Mum said, 'It won't last forever'
But I sulked in doubt.

At last, at last, the rain had stopped
My hopes were up to the top
It felt like one hundred degrees
I felt it would never end.

I couldn't believe it, I saw a rainbow
And I know the rain is coming again
Over the hills and across the glen.

Ruairi Gorman (9)
St Colman's Abbey Primary School, Newry

Rainy Day

When I wake up, I feel cold,
I look out of my window
To clouds of darkness.

Wet outside, trees blowing,
Gutters gushing,
Water running.

Then I walk outside
And it is like
Pins hitting my face.

I walk down the hill,
The wind hits me in the face
And knocks me down.

David McKevitt (10)
St Colman's Abbey Primary School, Newry

Van Der Sar

My favourite goalkeeper is Edwin Van der Sar
He really is such a star
One game he pulled off quite a stop
Out of all the saves, that one is the top!

From Fulham FC you were sold
You're a brilliant goalkeeper, although you're old
Better than the great Dida of Brazil
You even helped United to beat Liverpool, one-nil.

Ross Haughey (9)
St Colman's Abbey Primary School, Newry

My Weather Poem

The storm at night,
Gives me a fright,
Hailstones rattling on my roof,
Rain pelting at my window,
Wind whistling all around,
The heavy snow begins to fall,
Leaving footprints in my hall,
I put on my boots and coat,
Then go out to play,
In the slushy white snow.

Paul Curran (9)
St Colman's Abbey Primary School, Newry

Frog

Frog, frog, you drive my sister bananas,
With your green skin and your flipper feet, big eyes, no teeth,
When you get out, my parents go bonkers!

I'm so lucky to have a friend like you,
You're so lucky too,
You always escape death.

Like the time Dad almost stamped on you with his big feet,
But you bounced before you were dead meat,
We'll always have our differences,
But we'll be friends forever and ever.

Joshua O'Brien (9)
St Colman's Abbey Primary School, Newry

Creepy-Crawlies

Creepy-crawlies through the night,
Creepy-crawlies give you a fright,
Some are scary, some are not,
There's tarantulas and daddy-long-legs,
My auntie Jeanette is scared of the lot,
The flies are trapped in their prison cells,
Killed with the execution blade,
Their hairy bodies and eight legs,
Showing off their ugly heads.

Conall Keenan Reilly (9)
St Colman's Abbey Primary School, Newry

The Spider

He spins a web
At the corner of my wall
I do not know if it's a tarantula or not
But it's terror-full.

He's trying to get up on my bed
I say to my brain
I start shaking
Then look over my bed
He's dead!

Niall Grant (9)
St Colman's Abbey Primary School, Newry

Fletcher And The Stretcher

I don't like Darren Fletcher,
He was carried off on a stretcher,
When he went to take a free,
He slipped and broke his knee.

The spectators, they went crazy,
When he slipped over a daisy,
The physio, he ran out,
Just to give him a drink of stout.

Sure, the match was a disaster,
When Fletcher ended up in plaster,
The supporters, they'd had enough,
From their hero, who thought he was tough.

Garrett Campbell (10)
St Colman's Abbey Primary School, Newry

A Sunny Day

Sunny blue sky,
As hot as fire,
Sounds like sizzling bacon,
Melting tar on the roads,
Bees making honey,
From colourful flowers,
Happiness all around,
Oh, this summer's day!

Anthony McKeown (10)
St Colman's Abbey Primary School, Newry

My Dog Chico

My dog liked to play with footballs
He jumped high
I loved to pat him
And loved him sleeping on my bed.

Then he had to go to a farm
Mum sent my brother and me
To visit him and take him
Big buckets of food and water.

He was so funny
He loved me and I loved him
But he is gone now
I miss him.

Jonathan McEvoy (9)
St Colman's Abbey Primary School, Newry

Warm And Thirsty

What a lovely summer's day,
I am going out to play,
The sky is clear, the sun is strong,
People happy, strolling along.

I feel as hot as today,
I need a drink of water,
To help me go and play.

I had my drink straight from the sink,
The ice cream man is now here,
That's what I should eat while I relax,
On my summer seat.

Gary McAleavey (9)
St Colman's Abbey Primary School, Newry

My Pet Cat Buddy

My pet, Buddy, is very small,
He's only a kitten after all.
He chases birds,
He chases mice,
He must think they are all so nice.

He messes at night,
He nips and bites,
Sometimes he gives my mummy a fright.

When he gets out of the mud,
He's very muddy
And that's the story of my pet, Buddy.

Daniel McNulty (10)
St Colman's Abbey Primary School, Newry

Rainbow

Rainbow, rainbow, you are so bright
Rainbow, rainbow, I don't see you at night
Rainbow, rainbow, you're as pretty as a flower
Rainbow, rainbow, I see you after a rain shower
Rainbow, rainbow, you have lots of different colours
Rainbow, rainbow, I want you to stay forever and forever
Rainbow, rainbow, please never leave.

Rachel O'Shea (9)
St Davog's Primary School, Belleek

My Pet Coco

I have a little puppy,
She's brown and white,
She loves to cuddle up beside me at night.

Coco is her name,
Chasing is her game,
While I'm playing dolls,
Coco is chasing tennis balls.

Nessa Rooney (8)
St Davog's Primary School, Belleek

My Sister

Ciara is a baby, she is my sister
When I'm at school, I always miss her
I cannot wait until she can talk
I love to take her for a walk
Sometimes Ciara isn't happy
And then Mummy changes her nappy
Ciara smiles and laughs a lot
And when Ciara cries, she goes into her cot
Ciara drinks a lot of milk
And her skin feels like silk.

Kelly Louise Ferguson (8)
St Davog's Primary School, Belleek

I Love Football

Gaelic football and soccer I love to play,
I think about it night and day.
Six foot, seven inch, Peter Crouch strikes the ball,
Henry defends and saves it all
My favourite soccer teams are quite a few
Arsenal, Liverpool, Chelsea and Man U.

I go to Gaelic training all the time,
I run and run and get covered in grime.
But thoughts of Brewester, Cavanagh
And McDonald in Croke Park,
Keeps me going, from morning to dark.

Michael Óg McGarrigle (7)
St Davog's Primary School, Belleek

My Teacher

My teacher is funny,
My teacher is cool,
He really makes me enjoy school.
He teaches us English, maths and art,
But swimming is the best part.
His tea mug says 'I love beer',
I hope he teaches me every year.

Lauren Doogan (7)
St Davog's Primary School, Belleek

My House

D is for Daddy who I love and adore
A is for Andy, the boy next door
M is for Mammy who tucks me in at night
A is for around, it's a wonderful sight
N is for natural as it's stone all around
D is for décor as it's bright with sound
U is for unusual, for the taps that we have
S is for Shane who is football mad.

To other's, not much, to us, it's a lot,
That's 'Damandus', our home!

Caoimhe Rooney (8)
St Davog's Primary School, Belleek

Football Mad

I have two brothers, that is bad
Because they are football mad
Straight to the pitch after school
There to play for *Liverpool!*

They spend all their money on the kit
And all their time getting fit!
If their friends come to stay
They're made to kit out and go out to play.

This drives us all really crazy
And it's not as if we are that lazy
But every time they come from the pitch
We have to wash every dirty stitch!

Then one day, we'd had enough
We all decided to play tough!
When we saw the coast was clear
We swapped around all their gear!

Off they went for their game
Expecting things to be the same
But in their bag was something new
All their stuff was for *Man U!*

Joanne Murphy (8)
St Davog's Primary School, Belleek

My Granny

My granny is very kind
When I'm sick, Granny reads me a story
So I just say, never mind.
Granny comes to my house at night
Me and Granny sometimes go for walks
We go for a walk when there is some light.
Then all you can hear is us talk
Granny means so much to me
I will always love her.

Eve Rochfort (9)
St Davog's Primary School, Belleek

My Niece

My niece is so cute,
She giggles all day,
She is very playful
And loves to play.

Her name is Aoife,
Her surname is Kane,
She is very good,
There's no need to complain.

She is five months old,
She is growing every day,
She will be one-year-old,
On the 7th of May.

Arlene Cassidy (10)
St Davog's Primary School, Belleek

My Granny's Dog, Skippy

My granny's dog, Skippy, is black and white
She is very playful and very light
When we have an empty bottle
We throw it out the back
She goes flying out of the door
And gets ready to attack.

She has a little blue ball
She loves it the best of all
When we were little, we used to hide it
Then she could not find it.

She jumps about all the time
Except when I say a rhyme
Then she lies upon her paws
And there's no noise from her jaws.

She sometimes sits on my knee
I'm really scared that she will pee!
But I really like her a lot
She's the only dog I've got!

We love to take her for a run
We all have lots and lots of fun
She really is very nippy
That's my granny's dog, Skippy.

Aidan Murphy (10)
St Davog's Primary School, Belleek

My Granny

I love my granny, she's very good
She makes me lots of yummy food
When Daddy brings us all to stay
She always comes out with us to play.

She lives beside the railway track
The train runs right around the back
When we hear it going past
We run down the garden, very fast.

Sometimes she takes us for a walk
And along the way, we always talk
She shows us very interesting things
Like how some birds have different wings.

She's always cleaning after me
Cos I'm not as tidy as I should be
But with lots to do, she doesn't mind
That's because Granny is very kind.

Nights with her are always great
We're allowed to stay up late
In front of the fire, she tells us all
About the times when she was small.

When we have to go away
I really hate getting up that day
But Granny always stays in touch
I really love her, very much.

Conor Murphy (10)
St Davog's Primary School, Belleek

Hallowe'en

We go along an eerie path
The trees whisper
As we pass.

We hear scary sounds
Deafening cackles
Cauldrons boil
And other things crackle.

I split up from my friends
I'm scared and alone
Owls hoot
And I hear the werewolves tone.

Hallowe'en is here
People fear
They don't know
What it will bring this year.

Shane Edward Mimna (10)
St Davog's Primary School, Belleek

Hocus Pocus

Annoying and horrible
Totally intolerable!

Mummy hugger!
Who thinks it's as sweet as sugar.

Nose-picking brat
All ugly, like a rat!

Hocus pocus
This spell will make me a . . .

Boy!

Maeve Lunny (11)
St Davog's Primary School, Belleek

My Cats

I have owned a lot of cats,
Some of which are dead,
My favourite one is little Toots,
But she's too fond of bed!

I also have Fat Mamma,
She's a little on the chubby side,
I love to sit her by the fire,
But she'd rather be outside!

Then there is Sylvester,
He's the butch one of the pack,
He likes to show the rest who's boss,
But they laugh behind his back!

Last, there is my newest friend,
Who just yet hasn't got a name,
My gran says, 'Put it in a bag,'
But my kitten's not to blame!

There are lots more cats about the place
But they're not as nice as mine,
They squeal a lot and nick the food
And all night long they whine!

Cats, they're my favourite things!

Ethan McGrath (9)
St Davog's Primary School, Belleek

My Baby, Brad

My baby, Brad, is so cute
Even if he cries, I still love him
Even if he pulls my hair and makes me mad
He sometimes pulls my stuff and destroys things
But I still think he's good
I love him and spending time with him
'Cause he's the cutest baby in the whole wide world.

Nathan Hanley (9)
St Davog's Primary School, Belleek

Our House

It was the 18th of July, 2006
The day we up-rooted our sticks
Twelve months of hell
Is what my mum said
My dad nearly lost all his hair
There was me, there was Caoimhe
There was Mum and Dad
And we couldn't forget Holly, our cat
Where we were going, it wasn't far
Out in the country, not far from Belleek
But from where we were then
To where we are now
It's the place we now call our home.

Shane Rooney (9)
St Davog's Primary School, Belleek

My Sister

My sister is one year old
She never does what she is told
She has just learnt how to walk
But she has always known how to talk.

She loves to tear
And toddle up the stairs
When she sees the open door
She's determined even more.

Everyone thinks she's cute
But sometimes I wish she was mute!
And after all these things, I still love her
But if she didn't do all these things
I'd love her more!

Caoimhe McGarrigle (10)
St Davog's Primary School, Belleek

Football Mad

I love to play football, it makes me go mad
I bounce and kick and save
I love it when we win, but sometimes we lose
I love the free kicks, but the penalties are better
As the referee blows the whistle
And the manager roars and shouts on the sideline
We try to keep the ball out of the goal
And play our very best.

Peter Gilfedder (10)
St Davog's Primary School, Belleek

My Granny's Garden

My granny's garden has lots of flowers
And piles of muck in big, tall towers.
She loves her garden, lots and lots
And has pretty flowers in flowerpots.

She has a little dog called Boots,
Who likes to dig up flower roots.
She weeds all day on her hands and knees
And listens to the sounds of the buzzing bees.

My granny dislikes the slugs and snails
And all the dirt beneath her nails.
My granny's garden is her favourite place,
I know this by her smiling face!

Saoirse O'Loughlin (10)
St Davog's Primary School, Belleek

Spooky

Werewolves, bats, ghosts and rats
Howl and cry on Hallowe'en night
Creepy screams coming from witches.
Whooo coming from the nearby castle
Owls fly over the moon and scream in the cold
On Hallowe'en night.

JJ O'Brien (10)
St Martin's Primary School, Garrison

What . . . Is The Night?

The night is a big, black blanket
Spread across the sky.

It is a street
Filled with little lanterns.

The night is a bit of space
For all of us to see.

It is a place of wonder
Wherever I may be.

The night is a time of peace and quiet
In homes everywhere.

Fearghal Kelly (10)
St Martin's Primary School, Garrison

Dragons

D ragons roar, kill and eat, they only eat meat
R *umble! Rattle!* Here they come, watch your back, they could attack
A ttack! Attack! They will be back
G ood! I don't think so! Bad dragon! They're nasty beasts
O n my way back, they hit me with a sack
N ow they're gone, I hope they don't come back.

John Burns (9)
St Martin's Primary School, Garrison

Fantastic Friends

Fantastic friends are great
They are your best mates
We always have a good time
And we always feel fine

We like to play football
But sometimes we slip and fall
Being friends is great
Now I know we are the best of mates

We are the best of mates
We always feel great
We would not like to be a giraffe
But we would like to have a good laugh.

Aisling McGurl (8)
St Martin's Primary School, Garrison

Hallowe'en

Hallowe'en is coming near,
So you'd better fear,
Because the vampire will be here.

The witch will come,
All dressed in black,
On her broomstick, with her cat.

Children will come to your homes,
Please do not give them any bones,
But give them sweets for a treat!

Michelle Keegan-Rattcliff (9)
St Martin's Primary School, Garrison

Garrison!

Garrison is a lovely place to be,
There's some beautiful scenery.
We've got Lough Melvin,
So if you want to fish,
Come along for a tasty dish.

Please, come along to Garrison,
Have a drink in one of our friendly pubs,
Then have some tasty grub.

You can buy a television,
In Tony Keown's shop
And then go into Gilroy's
And shop till you drop.

Garrison is a lovely place to be
And really not too far from the sea,
I love Garrison, so will you
Because here in Garrison, the sky is blue.

Laura Keegan-Rattcliff (9)
St Martin's Primary School, Garrison

Earth!

Earth is a planet like a magnificent ball spinning around
It is like a doughnut without the hole in the middle
It is like my favourite ball my dad bought me last year
It is like a ball of cheerfulness spinning around and around
There's no fear - it's just a world
Spinning around and around and around!

Ciara McGrath (8)
St Martin's Primary School, Garrison

The Witch

The witch has nails as long as spears,
She even cries slimy tears.
Her eyes are the colour of red sweets,
Her hair is like red shoelaces.
She screams like a monkey,
She smells like a skunky.
She makes spells with spiders and slugs,
Sometimes she gives them hugs.

Connor Chappell (7)
St Martin's Primary School, Garrison

The Witch

The witch has nails as long as spears,
She even cries slimy tears.
Her eyes shine like horrible green grass,
Her hair grows like long weedy grass.
She screams like a cat,
She has horrible skin,
Her eyes are horrible and her legs looks like pins.

Oisin O'Brien (6)
St Martin's Primary School, Garrison

The Witch

The witch has nails as long as spears,
She even cries slimy tears.
Her eyes are hot red flames,
Her hair stands out like a bush.
She screams like a broken TV,
Her pet is a hairy spider.
She flies on a broom over my head.
She cooks bats and cats beside the fire,
Wherever she goes, her spell book is there.
Her name is Winnie,
She has a wart on her nose.
She thinks she's pretty,
But she is really very ugly.
Her hat is as black as a cat,
She loves money and a bit of honey,
She has really long, dirty toenails.

Katie Stewart (7)
St Martin's Primary School, Garrison

The Witch

The witch has nails as long as spears,
She even cries slimy tears.
Her eyes are like big, red diamonds,
Her hair is like big, fat worms.

Catie Wadsworth (7)
St Martin's Primary School, Garrison

The Witch

The witch has nails as long as spears,
She even cries slimy tears,
Her eyes are like dark red diamonds,
Her hair is black strips of mop,
She screams really squeaky,
Makes me feel very peaky,
She flies on her broomstick every day,
She makes her cat eat lumps of hay.

Chloe McGrath (6)
St Martin's Primary School, Garrison

The Witch

The witch has nails as long as spears,
She even cries slimy tears.
Her eyes shine like dark red diamonds,
Her hair is dark, as thick as black paint.
Green is the colour of her skin,
She screams like geese in winter,
Her house will need a painter.

Jonah Carty (7)
St Martin's Primary School, Garrison

The Witch

The witch has nails as long as spears,
She even cries slimy tears.
Her eyes are as blue as the sea
And I don't like it when she looks at me.
Her hair is as black as coal
And she screams just like a mole.
Her skin has bugs on it
And sometimes when she washes it,
The bugs go down the hole.
Her pet is a frog,
It likes to go in the bog.
She flies on her broomstick,
Everywhere.

Sinead McGurl (7)
St Martin's Primary School, Garrison

The Witch

The witch has nails as long as spears,
She even cries slimy tears,
Her eyes are diamonds, red,
She screams like a cat under the bed,
Her hair is rippling black as coal,
She flies on her broomstick,
Wherever she goes.

Cianna Treacy (7)
St Martin's Primary School, Garrison

The Witch

The witch has nails as long as spears
She even cries slimy tears.
Her eyes are red diamonds
Her hair is like black bags.

Lauren Timoney (6)
St Martin's Primary School, Garrison

The Witch

The witch has nails as long as spears
She even cries slimy tears
Her eyes are like red diamonds
Glowing in the day
Her hair looks like a ball of hay.

Tony Devine (7)
St Martin's Primary School, Garrison

The Witch

The witch has nails as long as spears
She even cries slimy tears
Her eyes are scary, green and sharp
Her hair is long and often damp
The witch is flying on her broom
She goes around from room to room.

Tristan Otto (7)
St Martin's Primary School, Garrison

My Monster

My monster has . . .
A body like a fuzzy coat
A nose like a small button
A mouth like a banana
Legs like breadsticks
And arms like a ruler

My monster is . . .
As friendly as a cat
As clever as a student
As loud as a tiger
As smelly as a skunk
As frightening as a ghost.

Lorena McIntyre (8)
St Martin's Primary School, Garrison

Monster House

My monster has . . .
A body like bones
Eyes like dead meat
A nose like cream
Legs like pencils
And arms like metal.

My monster is . . .
As friendly as a baby
As clever as a computer
As loud as a bomb
As smelly as a piglet
As frightening as thunder.

Jarlath O'Brien (8)
St Martin's Primary School, Garrison

Boredom

Boredom is dull
Boredom is uninteresting
Boredom is tiredness
Boredom is unimaginative
Boredom is going to bed when the sun is shining
Boredom is not fun.

Meghan McTernan (8)
St Martin's Primary School, Garrison

My Monster From Space

My monster has . . .
A body like wobbly jelly
Eyes like black ebony
A nose like a hairy button
A mouth like a blistered thumb
Legs like fat sausages
And arms like hard-boiled eggs.

My monster is . . .
As friendly as a princess
As clever as can be
As loud as a roaring lion
As smelly as stinky socks
As frightening as a tornado
My monster is called Stupo.

Mairéad Maguire (8)
St Martin's Primary School, Garrison

Tigers - Haiku

Tigers hunt their prey
Like speeding cars on the road
And soon their prey dies.

James Keown (8)
St Martin's Primary School, Garrison

Red

Red is anger
Red is a sign for stop
Red is the colour for berries
Red is the colour of curtains
Red is blood
Red is my favourite colour.

Darren Carson (8)
St Martin's Primary School, Garrison

My Monster

My monster has . . .
A body like slimy moss
Eyes like red blood
A nose like a spider's web
A mouth like a dragon's dungeon
Legs like tree trunks
And arms like a pterodactyl's wings.

My monster is . . .
As friendly as a kitten
As clever as a fox
As loud as an elephant
As smelly as a skunk
As frightening as a ghost.

Fiona Keegan (8)
St Martin's Primary School, Garrison

Red

Red is a raspberry
Red is a book
Red is a bright, new, shiny red car.

Red is anger
Red is blood
Red is fire.

Darragh Treacy (8)
St Martin's Primary School, Garrison

Red

Red like blood
Red like some cherries
Red like a red car
Red like some paint
Red like a heart
Red is my favourite colour.

Darragh Ferguson (8)
St Martin's Primary School, Garrison

Autumn

Animals collecting food for the winter,
Squirrels collecting nuts,
The nights are getting longer,
The days are getting shorter.

The leaves flutter down to the ground,
The leaves change colour,
Red, brown, yellow and orange,
Blackberries are growing on the hedges.

Ciaran McElroy (6)
St Mary's Primary School Dechomet, Castlewellan

Autumn

The birds go to a warmer country,
The berries grow on trees,
The leaves flutter off the trees,
The squirrels collect nuts.

It gets dark,
The farmers make wheat,
The nights are getting longer,
It is raining and the wind is getting stronger.

Cahal Owens (6)
St Mary's Primary School Dechomet, Castlewellan

Autumn

Squirrels collect nuts,
Leaves change colour,
Brown, red and yellow,
Pears growing on the trees,
Flowers start to die.

Farmers are harvesting their wheat,
Berries are red and black,
The nights are becoming longer,
The days are becoming shorter.

Katie Doyle (6)
St Mary's Primary School Dechomet, Castlewellan

Autumn

The leaves twirl and swirl in the breeze,
Berries start to grow on bushes,
The farmer is harvesting his fields,
Before it gets too cold.

Flowers start to die in the cold,
Leaves are changing colour,
Into red, orange, yellow and brown,
The nights are getting longer and colder.

Mollie Cunningham (6)
St Mary's Primary School Dechomet, Castlewellan

Autumn

Leaves fall off the trees
The squirrels collect their nuts
Berries grow on the bushes
Leaves change colour.

The birds go to a different country
All the animals collect their food
They sleep through autumn
The nights get longer.

Caoimhe Leneghan (6)
St Mary's Primary School Dechomet, Castlewellan

Autumn

Leaves fall off the trees,
Animals get ready to hibernate,
Birds fly away to a hot country,
Plums start to grow.

Flowers start to die,
Strong winds blow,
The nights get longer and longer,
The mornings get shorter and shorter.

Matthew Leneghan (6)
St Mary's Primary School Dechomet, Castlewellan

Autumn

The hedgehogs are making a nest in the leaves
To get ready to hibernate,
Leaves are changing colour
To red, yellow, orange and brown.

Red berries grow from the bushes,
Birds fly to a different country,
Farmers are harvesting crops,
The days are getting windy.

Tiarnan McEvoy (7)
St Mary's Primary School Dechomet, Castlewellan

Autumn

Now the birds are flying away,
Watch the squirrels coming out to play,
Leaves fluttering from the trees,
In a gentle, gentle breeze.

Leaves are changing colour
To red, yellow and brown,
The trees are in a lovely gown,
Red berries are growing along the lane,
We know autumn is here again.

Ciaran McElroy (7)
St Mary's Primary School Dechomet, Castlewellan

Autumn

Leaves fluttering in the sky
Leaves changing colour, brown, red, yellow and orange
The birds are flying away to a warmer country
The squirrels are collecting their nuts.

The flowers are dying
Berries are growing in the hedges
Autumn is here again
Farmers are harvesting fields.

Carlin Mooney (7)
St Mary's Primary School Dechomet, Castlewellan

My Friends

My friend are loving and caring
And always sharing
I will lend a helping hand
To any of my many friends.

School is fantastic play
Learning and having a laugh
The teachers are nice
With a bit of spice.

School is cool, Dechomet rules
And having fun in the sun
Is better than years ago
Here, everyone smiles
Better than the miseries of old.

Kathryn Kelly (10)
St Mary's Primary School Dechomet, Castlewellan

Autumn

The leaves flutter down to the ground
The leaves start to change to different colours
To brown and orange and yellow and red
The farmers start to cut their barley.

The animals start to hibernate
The berries start to grow in the hedges
The birds go to a different country
The nights are getting longer.

Claire Cunningham (7)
St Mary's Primary School Dechomet, Castlewellan

Autumn

Leaves are changing colour to brown, red, yellow and orange,
To warmer countries the birds are flying away,
Berries are growing in the hedges
Little squirrels come out to play.

The farmers are cutting the barley,
The leaves are fluttering down to the ground,
Animals are hibernating for the autumn,
Look at the nuts the squirrels have found.

Paul Savage (7)
St Mary's Primary School Dechomet, Castlewellan

Autumn

Colourful leaves fluttering down
Landing on the ground, making a colourful gown
As autumn goes by
The leaves are going to die.

The squirrels are nesting in the trees
There is a little breeze
The leaves are yellow, brown, orange and red
Some leaves are already dead.

Shaneen Owens (7)
St Mary's Primary School Dechomet, Castlewellan

Autumn

Colourful leaves fluttering in the breeze,
Cheeky squirrels nesting in the trees,
Red berries growing in my sight,
Everything is so bright.

When you walk by,
All the leaves just die,
Birds start to fly away,
I don't have much time to play.

Tiernan O'Rourke (7)
St Mary's Primary School Dechomet, Castlewellan

Autumn

Apple trees grow in orchards
Leaves fall off the trees
Squirrels collect nuts
Farmers harvest their crops.

The birds go to warmer countries
The leaves change colour
The berries grow in the hedges
The animals hibernate in the winter.

Pearse Davidson (7)
St Mary's Primary School Dechomet, Castlewellan

My Pup

I like my pup
Because he's small and cute
He is tan and white
With bright, shiny eyes.

He has little sharp teeth
And a black nose
His ears are spiky
With a little fat belly.

He jumps, he barks
He nibbles my toes
He follows me wherever I go
My little pup is called Febo.

Shea O'Boyle (8)
St Mary's Primary School Dechomet, Castlewellan

Autumn

The leaves are changing colour
The days are getting cool
The mild autumn breeze
Is gently blowing through the trees
While the leaves are falling to the ground
Crumbling, rustling, falling down
Autumn is here once more
I'm overjoyed, hear me roar!
Mystical colours all around me
I pick them up and throw them down.

Peirce Laverty (8)
St Mary's Primary School Dechomet, Castlewellan

Tractors

Tractors are big and powerful
Farmers used to use horses
But the only problem was
Before the horses could work
They had to be fed till they were full.

Now farmers use lots of makes of tractor
Fergie, Massey, Ford and many, many more
But I think the best of all, is the John Deere
They are bright yellow and green
And they make lots of noise
And can do lots of jobs.

I have two toy John Deeres
Which give me lots of fun
But the one I hate most of all
Is my grandad's silly Ford.

Conor McQuillan (8)
St Mary's Primary School Dechomet, Castlewellan

Autumn

Autumn is crisp leaves
I love playing in them so much.

Autumn is when animals hibernate
And birds migrate.

Autumn is when the farmer
Feeds the cows and puts them inside.

Autumn is juicy blackberries
Waiting to be eaten.

Autumn is short days
Nights getting longer.

Autumn mornings are misty
And dew is on the grass.

Caitlin Owens (8)
St Mary's Primary School Dechomet, Castlewellan

Autumn

Autumn is crunchy, crispy leaves
Waiting to fall off the trees.

Autumn is juicy blackberries
Being picked and eaten by people and birds.

Autumn is birds and animals
Migrating and hibernating.

Autumn is farmers
Harvesting and feeding the animals.

Autumn is shiny conkers
Being cracked.

Autumn is children
In warmer clothes.

Autumn is days
Getting shorter and nights longer.

Eve Cunningham (8)
St Mary's Primary School Dechomet, Castlewellan

Autumn

Red, yellow, orange and brown,
The ground is covered in a lovely gown,
The squirrels playing in the day,
The birds starting to fly away.

They flutter from the trees,
In the lovely, lovely breeze,
The berries are so bright,
They are a lovely sight.

Claire Greeran (8)
St Mary's Primary School Dechomet, Castlewellan

Autumn

The leaves are fluttering to the ground
Listen to the rustling sound
The leaves are starting to die
Stars are starting to twinkle in the sky.

Juicy red berries growing along the lane
Autumn is here once again
Birds are flying away
It's becoming too cold to stay.

Jane Doyle (8)
St Mary's Primary School Dechomet, Castlewellan

Our New Pup

Our new pup, Bailey, is black and white
She is nine weeks old
She likes to play a lot
She nibbles at everything.

Bailey loves to play in the garden
And runs about after me
She is a very playful animal
We got her from the kennels.

Bailey means the world to me
I love her so much
She plays with my other two dogs
I would never give her away.

Katie Rose Thornton (9)
St Mary's Primary School Dechomet, Castlewellan

Our Bales

Our bales are from golden straw fields
They have brilliant yields
We bring down the 45-foot trailer
In the field is a 'Welger' baler.

We strap them down tight
After all, they aren't light
Now onto the motorway to Louth
Straight home and into the cattle's mouths.

We're going back to Dundalk
Where all the bales are in stock
Now it's time to get more bales
Get back home and put them on sale.

James Savage (9)
St Mary's Primary School Dechomet, Castlewellan

My School Promise

Every day I will do my very best
And I won't do any less
My schoolwork will always please me
And I promise not to make a mess
I will colour very carefully
And keep my writing neat
I will always do my homework
And try hard on every test
I promise not to forget my promise
To do my very best.

Ryan Cunningham (9)
St Mary's Primary School Dechomet, Castlewellan

Squirrel

S quirrels are getting ready for a deep sleep
Q uarter of the acorns are left on the trees
U mbrellas are out for wet, cold and rainy days
I nside the bushes, there are lean, juicy blackberries
R oaring bonfires being lit everywhere around you
R obins are moving in very soon
E ntering the trees in the crackling leaves
L eaves are getting spread early in the afternoon.

PJ Davidson (9)
St Mary's Primary School Dechomet, Castlewellan

What Is Pink?

Pink is an animal
With a little twiggy tail
It is nothing
Like a big blue whale.
Pink is candyfloss
Sugary and sweet
It is not
Like a cold piece of meat.
School bags, lunch boxes
Covered in pink
My stress ball
Helps me to think.
Pink is a dress
With little pink shoes
If you entered a beauty contest
You would never lose.
Pink is a girl's colour
No doubt about it
But can you imagine
Living without it?

Paddy McEvoy (10)
St Mary's Primary School Dechomet, Castlewellan

What Is Yellow?

Yellow is happiness
Lovely and bright
Yellow are sunflowers
Which are a lovely sight.
Yellow is sweetcorn
A tiny bit sweet
Yellow is a banana
Nice to eat.
Sometimes yellow is custard
On your food
Yellow is not
Rude.
Yellow is a leopard
Prowling very fast
You know a leopard
Will never come last!

Aiden O'Hare (10)
St Mary's Primary School Dechomet, Castlewellan

What Is Green?

Green is the grass
Spiky and strong
Green is a dinosaur
Hopping along.
Green is the Ireland flag
And white and gold
Sometimes green is the Leitrim team
We use green thread when we tear a seam!
Green is a turtle
Mischievous and bold
Green is an alien, slimy and green
When their spaceship flies, there is a green beam.
I like green!

Sean Óg O'Rourke (10)
St Mary's Primary School Dechomet, Castlewellan

Aaron's Poem

A utumn is near and we all cheer
A ll the leaves fall off the trees
R obins are getting ready for winter
O ctober is almost here
N o more playing in the sun
S ummer has gone to bed

P eople are getting ready for Hallowe'en
O utdoor games are over
E venings are getting shorter
M ornings are getting darker.

Aaron Owens (10)
St Mary's Primary School Dechomet, Castlewellan

Autumn

Autumn comes
With cracking conkers
Autumn comes
With fog and frost
Autumn comes
With a blaze of colour
Autumn comes
With big bonfires
Autumn comes
With fireworks
Autumn comes
With leaves all over
Autumn comes
With Hallowe'en.

Peter McEvoy (10)
St Mary's Primary School Dechomet, Castlewellan

What Is Green?

Green is a lime
Lovely and sweet
Green is a melon
Which I like to eat.
Green is Ireland
A lovely place
Green can be Celtic
They have teams to face.
Sometimes green
Is a dirty nose
Green is a smell
In-between your toes.
Green is a snake
All silky and smooth
Green is a crocodile
That will quickly move.
Green is a mountain
Which I like to climb
Green is a shamrock
Or it could be thyme.

Shana O'Boyle (10)
St Mary's Primary School Dechomet, Castlewellan

What Is Orange?

Orange is the sunset
Nice and bright
Orange are the leaves
Blazing in the light.
Sometimes orange is a parrot
Chirping all day
Talking nonsense
Whatever it is trying to say.
Orange is a JCB
Driving up the road
Maybe a circus tent
Entertaining quite a load.
Orange is the icing on a birthday cake
Delicious to eat
Just like oranges
Sour and sweet.

Claren Owens (10)
St Mary's Primary School Dechomet, Castlewellan

What Is Yellow?

Yellow is the sand,
Soft and smooth,
Yellow is a banana,
With its curves and grooves.
Sometimes yellow,
Can be ice cream,
There's the colour yellow,
In the Antrim team.
Yellow is a lemon,
Sour and sweet,
Juicy and bitter,
It is difficult to eat!
Yellow is a milkshake,
That tastes nice,
Yellow is a cat,
Who likes to chase mice.
Sometimes yellow can be hay,
You can see the chicks
On a spring day.

Megan Owens (10)
St Mary's Primary School Dechomet, Castlewellan

Hedgehog In Autumn

H edgehog collecting leaves for winter
E asily walking under his pile
D umping the leaves down
G radually getting sleepier
E asing his hunger
H e eats the food
O ut he goes because it is summer
G reeting all his friends

I n comes the autumn again
N one of the leaves have fallen though

A ll there are
U nder the trees, are conkers and clover
T here he makes his bed
U p in a hole at the bottom of the tree
M ade of clover and conkers
N ow he is safe there, he is happy.

Natasha McQuillan (10)
St Mary's Primary School Dechomet, Castlewellan

What Is Yellow?

Yellow is a milkshake
That tastes very good
Yellow is a chick
That likes to eat food.
Yellow is the sand
Soft under your feet
Yellow is sweetcorn
That is lovely to eat.
Sometimes yellow
Is custard
It tastes really different
To mustard.
Yellow is a bruise
That is very sore
Yellow is vanilla ice cream
Of which I want more!
Yellow is like amber
That gets us ready
Yellow is hay
That you stack steady.

Erin Leneghan (11)
St Mary's Primary School Dechomet, Castlewellan

Autumn Life

Autumn is finally here,
Hip hip hooray is what we cheer,
Dormice getting ready to hibernate
And swallows starting to migrate.
Mr Blackbird's heading south,
With a berry in his mouth,
All the cows are coming in,
Jumping in the leaves, what a din!
The trees are bare,
We're taking in the mare,
Freaky masks on Hallowe'en,
The wicked witch is the ugliest queen!
Leaves are fluttering down,
Forming a lovely gown,
Goodbye summer, see you soon.

Michael O'Rourke (11)
St Mary's Primary School Dechomet, Castlewellan

Molly McLeading

(Inspired by 'Ella McStumping' by M Dugan)

Molly McLeading
Was fond of reading
By bookshelves and chairs
Even on the stairs.
She would have a look
Then read the whole book.
At the age of four
She fell through the door
And with a mighty scream
She fell flat like fresh cream.
Doctor McNurse
Said, 'She'll get worse'
'She can go home next day.'
The hospital say
And Molly McLeading
Has given up reading.

Sarah Sim (10)
The Irish Society's Primary School, Coleraine

Sarah McTriding

(Inspired by 'Ella McStumping' by M Dugan)

Sarah McTriding
Was fond of riding
On beaches and hills
Forests and by mills
If she went home
She'd come back for more
At the age of six
Her horse had been fixed
She fell into a tree
And fractured her knee
Doctor Toking
Was not joking
Mr Nome
Said, 'She'll come home'
And Sarah McTriding
Has given up riding.

Rebecca Sim (10)
The Irish Society's Primary School, Coleraine

McDonald's! McDonald's!

(Inspired by 'Spaghetti, Spaghetti!' by J Prelutsky)

McDonald's! McDonald's!
You have wonderful stuff,
I love you, McDonald's,
I can't get enough!
Your fries are so tasty,
Your burgers are fine,
McDonalds, McDonald's,
I wish you were mine!

McDonald's! McDonald's!
McFlurries are yummy,
Chicken nuggets are scrummy,
I love Big Macs!
A nice big meal from McDonald's,
All over my plate,
McDonald's, McDonald's,
I think you are great!

McDonald's! McDonald's!
I love you a lot,
You're yummy, so scrummy,
Delicious and hot,
I gobble you down,
I can't get enough,
McDonald's, McDonald's,
You have wonderful stuff!

Charlotte Warke (10)
The Irish Society's Primary School, Coleraine

Jenny McSying

(Inspired by 'Ella McStumping' by M Dugan)

Jenny McSying
Was fond of flying
She flew to Peru
And went to the zoo
She would fly in the air
With such a flare
At the age of thirteen
She was going to be seen
Jumping from a plane
We thought she was insane
Doctor McBurse
Said, 'She'll get worse'
The hospital said
'She'll have to stay in bed'
Jenny McSying
Doesn't like flying!

Hayley Gibson (10)
The Irish Society's Primary School, Coleraine

Rachael McPooping

(Inspired by 'Ella McStumping' by M Dugan)

Rachael McPooping
Was fond of cooking
From books to spooks
She looked for cooks
When she finished cooking the boar
She decided to make some more
At the age of two
She needed the loo
When her food didn't sell
She let out a yell
Doctor McSnutid
Said, 'She's stupid'
The patient said
'She'll never stay'
And Rachael McPooping
Has given up cooking.

Shareffa Walker (10)
The Irish Society's Primary School, Coleraine

Chocolate! Chocolate!

(Inspired by 'Spaghetti, Spaghetti!' by J Prelutsky)

Chocolate! Chocolate!
You're wonderful stuff
I love you, oh chocolate
I can't get enough
White chocolate Kit-Kat
Melted, oh please
Chocolate! Chocolate!
Give me some, please!

Chocolate! Chocolate!
Piled high in a mound
You're so delicious
But you make my stomach round!
Chocolate! Chocolate!
I love you a lot
I can't get enough
Oh, you're wonderful stuff!

Sarah Young (10)
The Irish Society's Primary School, Coleraine

Billy McLinging

(Inspired by 'Ella McStumping' by M Dugan)

Billy McLinging
Was fond of singing
In a car
And in a bar
In a barn
And down in Larne
At the age of four
He sung more and more
So some guy from the south
Said, 'Close your mouth!'
Doctor McGet
Said, 'He's upset'
The hospital said
'Stay in bed'
And Billy McLinging
Has given up singing.

Adam Gellatly (11)
The Irish Society's Primary School, Coleraine

Hannah McDreaming

(Inspired by 'Ella McStumping' by M Dugan)

Hannah McDreaming
Was fond of cleaning
From upstairs to downstairs
To bookshelves and chairs
She would mop the floor
And dust the door
At the age of three
She wiped the TV
With one mighty cloth
She killed a poor moth
Doctor McLurse
Said, 'She'll get worse'
And the hospital say
'She can't clean today'
And Hannah McDreaming
Has given up cleaning.

Jordan Moore (11)
The Irish Society's Primary School, Coleraine

Amy McLating

(Inspired by 'Ella McStumping' by M Dugan)

Amy McLating
Was fond of skating
From ranks and planks
To the ground and all around
She would skate to the sky
And would never lie
At the age of eight
She went through the gate
With one mighty blade
She saw herself fade
Doctor McPumping
Said, 'Her heart was thumping'
And the hospital said
'Get her away'
Amy McLating
Has given up skating.

Demi Quinn (10)
The Irish Society's Primary School, Coleraine

Strawberries

(Inspired by 'Spaghetti, Spaghetti!' by J Prelutsky)

Strawberries, strawberries
You're wonderful stuff
I love you strawberries
I can't get enough
You're covered with sauce
And you're juicy inside
Strawberries, strawberries
I eat you with pride.

Strawberries, strawberries
I love you a lot
You're squishy, you're squashy
Delicious and when I gobble you down
Oh, I can't get enough
Strawberries, strawberries
You're wonderful stuff!

Abigail Sharp (10)
The Irish Society's Primary School, Coleraine

Jack McFating

(Inspired by 'Ella McStumping' by M Dugan)

Jack McFating
Was fond of skating
He skated round the house
And ran over a mouse
He skated from here to there
He skated everywhere
At the age of eight
He got his first skate
One day he was late
And fell off a gate
Doctor McLetter
Said, 'He'll get better'
He had a scare
And pulled out his hair
So Jack McFating
Has given up skating.

Jack Friel (10)
The Irish Society's Primary School, Coleraine

Fergie McMing-Ming

(Inspired by 'Ella McStumping' by M Dugan)

Fergie McMing-Ming
Was fond of singing
From concerts to stages
CDs to pages
She could sing all night
She could sing alright
At the age of fifteen
She was a pop queen
To win their hearts
She had to hit the charts
Doctor McPry
Said, 'She'll die'
But the hospital say
'She can come back next May'
And Fergie McMing-Ming
Has given up singing.

Danni Millar (11)
The Irish Society's Primary School, Coleraine

Sarah McGlancing

(Inspired by 'Ella McStumping' by M Dugan)

Sarah McGlancing
Was fond of dancing
Around stages and floors
Fountains and doors
She could dance around
Without a sound
At the age of eight
She could dance over a gate
She danced and fell
And said, 'Farewell'
But Doctor McFiv
Said, 'She'll live'
The hospital say
'She can go home the next day'
Sarah McGlancing
Has given up dancing!

Olivia Clarke (10)
The Irish Society's Primary School, Coleraine

Bradley McFunning

(Inspired by 'Ella McStumping' by M Dugan)

Bradley McFunning
Was fond of running
From place to place
He won his race
He would run to the car
And run really far
At the age of eight
He ran through the gate
He ran to get his tea
But bumped into a tree
Doctor McLive
Said, 'He'll survive'
And then he said
'You were nearly dead'
Bradley McFunning
Has given up running.

Bradley Dempster (10)
The Irish Society's Primary School, Coleraine

Cookies! Cookies!

(Inspired by 'Spaghetti, Spaghetti!' by J Prelutsky)

Cookies! Cookies!
You're wonderful stuff
I love you cookies
I can't get enough
You're covered with milk
And you're sprinkled with choc
Cookies! Cookies
Oh, give me some, please!

Cookies! Cookies!
Piled high with biscuit!
You melt your chocolate
You move around my mind
There are chocolate cookies
All over my face
Cookies! Cookies!
I think you're great!

Cookies! Cookies!
I love you a lot
You're milky, you're chocolatey
Delicious and sometimes hot
I gobble you down
Oh, I can't get enough
Cookies! Cookies!
You're wonderful stuff!

Aaruj Akbar (11)
The Irish Society's Primary School, Coleraine

Melissa McFlinging

(Inspired by 'Ella McStumping' by M Dugan)

Melissa McFlinging
Was fond of singing
In school and at home
On her fashionable phone
Melissa would sing all day and night
And sing to her teacher and give her a fright
At the age of eight
She walked into a gate
And had a very terrible fate
Doctor McHoice said
'She might lose her voice'
And Melissa McFlinging
Has given up singing.

Rachael Thompson (11)
The Irish Society's Primary School, Coleraine

Figgy McFitching

(Inspired by 'Ella McStumping' by M Dugan)

Figgy McFitching
Was fond of twitching
When happy or sad
Angry or mad
He'd twitch to Peru
Then go to the loo
At the age of ten
He twitched up Big Ben
In a state of shock
He began to rock
To and fro
With nowhere to go
He began to cry
But didn't know why
Doctor McFrown
Said, 'He'll never get down'
The hospital say
'They'll get him down some way'
And Figgy McFitching
Has given up twitching.

Mahnoor Tughral (11)
The Irish Society's Primary School, Coleraine

Harry McWeeding

(Inspired by 'Ella McStumping' by M Dugan)

Harry McWeeding
Was fond of reading
From libraries to bookstores
And reading about wars
He would read all the way
Until the end of the day
At the age of four
He walked into a door
With a bang on the door
He fell to the floor
Doctor McDine
Said, 'He'll be fine'
And the hospital say
'He can't come today'
And Harry McWeeding
Has given up reading.

Jade McMaster (10)
The Irish Society's Primary School, Coleraine

Teddy! Oh Teddy!

(Inspired by 'Spaghetti, Spaghetti!' by J Prelutsky)

Teddy! Oh Teddy!
You're wonderful stuff
I love you, oh Teddy
I can't get enough
You're covered with fur
And stuffed up with fluff
Teddy! Oh Teddy!
Oh, give me a hug!

Teddy! Oh Teddy!
Held in my arms
You cuddle, you huddle
You stick around
There's Teddy fluff
All over my face
Teddy! Oh Teddy!
I think you are great!

Teddy! Oh Teddy!
I love you a lot
You're soft, you're fluffy
Cuddly and fluffy
I hug you all over
Oh, I can't get enough.

John Gordon (11)
The Irish Society's Primary School, Coleraine

Sarah McShowning

(Inspired by 'Ella McStumping' by M Dugan)

Sarah McShowning
Was fond of moaning
In supermarkets and in her house
She would even scare a mouse
She would moan dawn till dusk
She wouldn't stop to touch an elephant tusk
At the age of two
She threw a shoe
With all her might
She would always fight
Dr Spudnik
Said, 'She's frantic'
The nurses said, 'She's mad'
Now Sarah was sad
So Sarah McShowning
Was still moaning.

Tori Cameron (11)
The Irish Society's Primary School, Coleraine

Mr McBlue

(Inspired by 'Ella McStumping' by M Dugan)

Mr McBlue
Was fond of glue
He stuck it everywhere
Including over everyone's hair
Their hair smelt like moss
And they were very *cross!*
At the age of ten
He had no friends
Because he put glue in their ears
Which made them not hear
Doctor Bic
Said, 'They'd be sick'
Gave them some pills
Without a bill
And Mr McBlue
Has given up sticking glue!

Duncan Chapman (10)
The Irish Society's Primary School, Coleraine

Fireworks

Fireworks are very bright
Fizzing like a can of Sprite
Jumping like ten kangaroos
Whizzing like a monkey in a zoo
Swooping like a bird of prey
Screaming like a roaring bay
Fireworks are good on a dark day.

Jonathan Kennedy (10)
The Irish Society's Primary School, Coleraine

Nicholas McBing

(Inspired by 'Ella McStumping' by M Dugan)

Nicholas McBing
Was fond of the king
He dressed up like one
But couldn't do a sum
He bought his own crown
And he didn't like to frown
At the age of three
He looked like you and me
But after that
He wanted a cat
Doctor McUre
Said, 'There's no cure'
And walked out the door
With dirt on the floor
And Nicholas McBing
Has given up being king.

Faine Eustace (11)
The Irish Society's Primary School, Coleraine

Emma McCoking

(Inspired by 'Ella McStumping' by M Dugan)

Emma McCoking
Was fond of smoking
She liked to smoke
With her friend, Coke
They smoked everywhere
And anywhere they went
At the age of eleven
She was nearly sent to Heaven
Coughing and choking
But she was still smoking
Doctor Mouse
Said, 'Come to her house'
Explaining to her folks
Why she shouldn't smoke
And now Emma McCoking
Has given up smoking.

Cara Ferguson (11)
The Irish Society's Primary School, Coleraine

Rachel McKay

(Inspired by 'Ella McStumping' by M Dugan)

Rachel McKay
Was fond of pie
She ate them on the train
And even on the plane
Then one night she ran out of pie
So she went to her room to cry
At the age of six
She felt sick
She thought she might have eaten
Too much before sleeping
Doctor Wray
Said, 'She'll pay
But she'll get better
After a bit of good weather'
And now Rachel McKay
Has given up pie.

Hannah Gibson (10)
The Irish Society's Primary School, Coleraine

George McLispeys

(Inspired by 'Ella McStumping' by M Dugan)

George McLispeys
Was fond of Rice Krispies
He ate them with milk
While wearing silk
He ate them on the plane
With his brother, Shane
At the age of three
He ate them up the tree
One day he fell
And then he wasn't well
Doctor Shren
Told him not to eat them
Only at the table
While his mum told him fables
And now George McLispeys
Has given up Rice Krispies.

Sarah Boyles (10)
The Irish Society's Primary School, Coleraine

Pasta! Pasta!

Pasta! Pasta!
I got it from Asda
Pasta! Pasta!
I eat it in my Mazda
I love it so much
I crunch and munch
Pasta! Pasta
It makes me faster
I take it with beef
I take it with cheese
It gets stuck in my teeth
When I'm asleep
Next morning I pull
And out it comes
With lots and lots
And lots of teeth!

Reuben Simpson (10)
The Irish Society's Primary School, Coleraine

Cocktail Sausages!

(Inspired by 'Spaghetti, Spaghetti!' by J Prelutsky)

Cocktail sausages! Cocktail sausages!
You're so small and great
You've got a super taste
Cocktail sausages! Cocktail sausages!

Cocktail sausages! Cocktail sausages!
You're a good, good mate
And I love you on my plate
Cocktail sausages! Cocktail sausages!

Cocktail sausages! Cocktail sausages!
You sizzle and bang
And in the pan you clang
Cocktail sausages! Cocktail sausages!

Jamie Rosborough (10)
The Irish Society's Primary School, Coleraine

Megan McDowns

(Inspired by 'Ella McStumping' by M Dugan)

Megan McDowns
Was fond of pounds
She liked the gold
That wasn't old
She knew she was rich
But so did the snitch
At the age of four
She wanted more
She was in pain
Because she'd put her hand down a drain
Doctor McDane
Said, 'What a we'an
She'll be better soon'
Then she saw the moon
And Megan McDowns
Has given up pounds.

Megan Downs (10)
The Irish Society's Primary School, Coleraine

Naomi McWraying

(Inspired by 'Ella McStumping' by M Dugan)

Naomi McWraying
Was fond of playing
She played with socks
And then with rocks
Stones and rings
And bricks and twigs
At the age of five
She found a beehive
She showed her friend, Derick
He went hysteric
Doctor Macauley
Said, 'At least she is jolly'
But her dad had to forbid
Her playing with kids
And Naomi McWraying
Has given up playing.

Naomi Hazel Wray (10)
The Irish Society's Primary School, Coleraine

Sweets!

(Inspired by 'Spaghetti, Spaghetti!' by J Prelutsky)

Sweets! Sweets!
Wonderful sweets
Scrummy and yummy
I can't get too many
Chocolate and toffees
Vanilla and strawberries.

Sweets! Sweets!
I love you a lot
You're chewy and sticky
They stick in my teeth
Please give me some more!

Sweets! Sweets!
In a box, in a packet
Or not at all
Lovely and sweet
All of them to eat
Take one at a time
They'll last longer then
Piled high to the sky.

Clarice Friel (10)
The Irish Society's Primary School, Coleraine

Grapes

(Inspired by 'Spaghetti, Spaghetti!' by J Prelutsky)

Grapes! Grapes!
Lie on my plate
I love you, grapes
You look like apes
Grapes! Grapes!
You look so great
You're at the top of my rate
Come onto my plate!

Yasmin Macauley (11)
The Irish Society's Primary School, Coleraine

Emma McClarke

(Inspired by 'Emma McStumping' by M Dugan)

Emma McClarke
Was fond of the dark
As soon as that
She was out like a cat
She dreamt of the sun
But she was very, very dumb
At the age of three
She dreamt of a tree
She dreamt of the pool
The doctor said that she was ill
And she should stay on the pill
She awoke in the dark
With a lot of Clarkes
And Emma McClarke
Has given up the dark!

Emma Clarke (10)
The Irish Society's Primary School, Coleraine

Chocolate! Chocolate!

(Inspired by 'Spaghetti, Spaghetti!' by J Prelutsky)

Chocolate! Chocolate!
You taste so sweet
You're one in a million
And you're nice to eat.

You melt in my mouth
You couldn't taste better
I'll eat you in my house
And leave none for the mouse
Chocolate! Oh chocolate!
Oh! Oh! Oh!

Amy Taylor (10)
The Irish Society's Primary School, Coleraine

Chips! Chips! Chips!

(Inspired by 'Spaghetti, Spaghetti!' by J Prelutsky)

Chips! Chips!
You're wonderful things
Yellow on the outside
White on the inside.

Chips! Chips!
You're stuffed with fat
Chips! Chips!
You're so fat
Big, small, whatever you are
Chips! Chips!
I'll eat you with sauce
I couldn't survive without you
I love chips!

Victoria Irwin (11)
The Irish Society's Primary School, Coleraine

Spazzy McMinnis

(Inspired by 'Ella McStumping' by M Dugan)

Spazzy McMinnis
Was fond of Guinness
He got himself drunk
Turned into a punk
Stabbed his wife
Used a sharp knife
At the age of seven
He drank to high Heaven
He woke up in bed
With a thumping head
Doctor McPick
Said he was very sick
And since all that pain
Nothing has been to his gain
Spazzy McMinnis
Has given up Guinness!

Alex Skuce (10)
The Irish Society's Primary School, Coleraine

Andy McWarding

(Inspired by 'Ella McStumping' by M Dugan)

Andy McWarding
Was fond of boarding
Shelves and stairs
Tables and chairs
He would ride through the halls
End up on the walls
At the age of ten
He jumped over Big Ben
He glided over the clock
Just as it went *tick-tock*
Doctor Hawk
Said he'd just got a knock
When he came round
His board was not to be found
And Andy McWarding
Has given up boarding.

Stephen Coulter (11)
The Irish Society's Primary School, Coleraine

Bruce McNorris

(Inspired by 'Ella McStumping' by M Dugan)

Bruce McNorris
Was fond of the forest
Then one day he found a key
And showed it to his mum
Then his mum said to him
'Don't lose that golden key'
At the age of three
He lost the key up a tree
So he went to get the golden key
But before he did, he broke his knee
Doctor McGee said to him
'Don't you climb anymore trees
Or else I will have to saw off your knees'
When he got home, he lay in front of the TV
And so Bruce McNorris
Has given up going to the forest.

Andrew William Coulter (11)
The Irish Society's Primary School, Coleraine

Fireworks

Fireworks are fan-diddly-tastic
Fizzing like Coke which tastes unlike boke
Jumping like a kangaroo that needs the loo
Whizzing like a drunken wink looking for something pink
Whirling like a helicopter ready to go for a flopper
Swooping like a murderous eagle going to annoy a Beagle
Screaming like a goth with a helpless moth
Fireworks are fan-diddly-tastic!

Jakob Henry Gault Allen (10)
The Irish Society's Primary School, Coleraine

Fireworks

Fireworks are fantastic shooting stars
Fizzing like cans of Fanta squirting on Mars
Jumping like speeding cars with chocolate bars
Whizzing like tingly sours
Whirling like water going down a plug for hours
Swooping like tomato ketchup on chips
Screaming like granny when she hurts her hips
Fireworks are fantastic shooting stars!

Kurtis Thompson (10)
The Irish Society's Primary School, Coleraine

Fireworks

Fireworks are spectacular
Fizzing like Coke from the Burger King
Jumping like me on a pogo stick
Whizzing like aeroplanes
Whirling like an eagle in the sky
Swooping like a hang-glider in the sky
Screaming like my sister watching a movie
Zooming like a Ferrari Enzo.

Peter Culkin (10)
The Irish Society's Primary School, Coleraine

Fireworks

Fireworks are good fun
Fizzing like Coca-Cola
Jumping like a mad kangaroo
Whizzing like a burning sparkler
Whirling like a spinning top
Swooping like an eagle ready to catch its prey
Screaming like a little girl who saw a spider
Fireworks are excellent fun!

Matthew Thomas Wisener (10)
The Irish Society's Primary School, Coleraine

Fireworks

Fireworks are colourful
Fizzing like cola
Jumping like a jack-in-the-box
Whizzing like a boomerang
Whirling like a waterwheel
Swooping like an eagle
Screaming like young children
Fireworks are great!

Joel Stanbridge (11)
The Irish Society's Primary School, Coleraine

Fireworks

Fireworks are incredibly awesome
Fizzing like lemonade
Jumping like kamikaze kangaroos
Whizzing like horrible hurricanes
Whirling like terrible typhoons
Swooping like crazy roller coasters
Screaming like fed-up girls
Zooming like F1 cars
Fireworks are amazing!

Kate Hewitt (10)
The Irish Society's Primary School, Coleraine

Fireworks

Fireworks are all different colours
Fizzing like Coke or Fanta maybe
Jumping like frogs or toads and things
Whizzing like some rides in Barry's
Whirling like mini tabletop spinners
Swooping like an eagle down on prey
Screaming like my brother when he's mad
Fireworks are the most wonderful things!

Sarah Henning (11)
The Irish Society's Primary School, Coleraine

Fireworks

Fireworks are cool
Fizzing like Red Bull
Jumping like you would on a pogo stick
Whizzing like a ride that makes you really sick
Whirling like a cyclone
Swooping like a dog on a bone
Screaming like a child
Fireworks are wild!

Jenny Clarke (10)
The Irish Society's Primary School, Coleraine

Fireworks

Fireworks are so bright
Fizzing like a bottle of Sprite
Jumping, jumping really far
Whizzing like a sports car
Whirling like a spinning hoop
Swooping like a monkey through a loop
Screaming like a baby who wants to be fed
Fireworks make me jump out of my bed!

James Hemphill (10)
The Irish Society's Primary School, Coleraine

Fireworks

Fireworks are like coloured ink
Fizzing like my favourite drink
Jumping like a crazed kangaroo
Whizzing like a car at 102
Whirling like a whirlpool in the sea
Swooping like a monkey in a tree
Screaming like a newborn babe
Fireworks, better stand back if they're in a cave!

Shane McMullan (11)
The Irish Society's Primary School, Coleraine

Envy

Envy sneaks up towards my ear,
She whispers with her green locks of hair,
'You wish you were as beautiful as me?
Well, I am sorry, you can't be me!'
I say, 'Why do you think you are so beautiful?
All you have is green locks of hair.'

Envy tries to hide
In the corner of my eye
Still whispering to herself,
'I am, I am, you're not, you're not.'

Hayley McMullan (10)
The Irish Society's Primary School, Coleraine

Meeting The Feelings

Concern tiptoed up to me, through the shadows she advanced,
She stared me in the eye, her eyebrows raised
And in a quiet voice she said,
'Are you alright? You look quite sad! Please tell me
And I'll make you glad!'
Now it was *my* turn to look *her* in the eye.
I raised *my* eyebrows and stepped sideways away,
I look back and see her eyes water and her bottom lip quiver,
Whoops! Maybe I should have answered her!

Desperation ran towards me, splashing through the puddles,
She widened her eyes and said in a trembling voice,
'Help me, help me! I'm down on my knees! I'm begging you, please!'
Wow! Nothing like this has happened before!
I patted her on the head but paid no heed,
I walked away into the silent street. She followed me,
Oh well, now I have a follower.

Claire Cooper (11)
The Irish Society's Primary School, Coleraine